PLANTING THE TREES OF KENYA

THE STORY OF WANGARI MAATHAI

Claire A. Nivola

Frances Foster Books

Farrar, Straus and Giroux / New York

As Wangari Maathai tells it, when she was growing up on a farm in the hills of central Kenya, the earth was clothed in its dress of green.

Fig trees, olive trees, crotons, and flame trees covered the land, and fish filled the pure waters of the streams.

The fig tree was sacred then, and Wangari knew not to disturb it, not even to carry its fallen branches home for firewood. In the stream near her homestead where she went to collect water for her mother, she played with glistening frogs' eggs, trying to gather them like beads into necklaces, though they slipped through her fingers back into the clear water.

Her heart was filled with the beauty of her native Kenya when she left to attend a college run by Benedictine nuns in America, far, far from her home. There she studied biology, the science of living things. It was an inspiring time for Wangari. The students in America in those years dreamed of making the world better. The nuns, too, taught Wangari to think not just of herself but of the world beyond herself.

How eagerly she returned to Kenya! How full of hope and of all that she had learned!

She had been away for five years, only five years, but they might have been twenty—so changed was the landscape of Kenya.

Wangari found the fig tree cut down, the little stream dried up, and no trace of frogs, tadpoles, or the silvery beads of eggs. Where once there had been little farms growing what each family needed

to live on and large plantations growing tea for export, now almost all the farms were growing crops to sell. Wangari noticed that the people no longer grew what they ate but bought food from stores. The store food was expensive, and the little they could afford was not as good for them as what they had grown themselves, so that children, even grownups, were weaker and often sickly.

She saw that where once there had been richly wooded hills with grazing cows and goats, now the land was almost treeless, the woods gone. So many trees had been cut down to clear the way for more farms that women and children had to walk farther and farther in search of firewood to heat a pot or warm the house. Sometimes they walked for hours before they found a tree or bush to cut down. There were fewer and fewer trees with each one they cut, and much of the land was as bare as a desert.

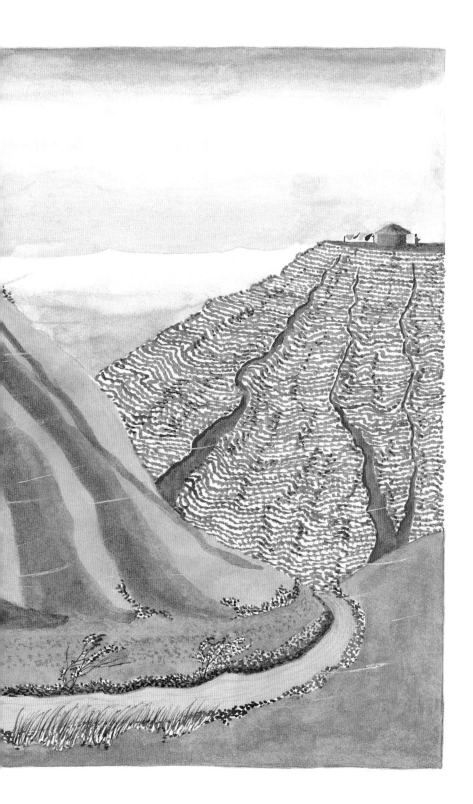

Without trees there were no roots to hold the soil in place. Without trees there was no shade. The rich topsoil dried to dust, and the "devil wind" blew it away. Rain washed the loose earth into the once-clear streams and rivers, dirtying them with silt.

"We have no clean drinking water," the women of the countryside complained, "no firewood to cook with. Our goats and cows have nothing to graze on, so they make little milk. Our children are hungry, and we are poorer than before."

Wangari saw that the people who had once honored fig trees and now cut them down had forgotten to care for the land that fed them. Now the land, weak and suffering, could no longer take care of the people, and their lives became harder than ever.

The women blamed others, they blamed the government, but Wangari was not one to complain. She wanted to do something. "Think of what we ourselves are doing," she urged the women. "We are cutting down the trees of Kenya.

"When we see that we are part of the problem," she said, "we can become part of the solution."

She had a simple and big idea.

"Why not plant trees?" she asked the women.

She showed them how to collect tree seeds from the trees that remained. She taught them to prepare the soil, mixing it with manure. She showed them how to wet that soil, press a hole in it with a stick, and carefully insert a seed. Most of all she taught them to tend the growing seedlings, as if they were babies, watering them twice a day to make sure they grew strong.

It wasn't easy. Water was always hard to come by. Often the women had to dig a deep hole by hand and climb into it to haul heavy bucketfuls of water up over their heads and back out of the hole. An early nursery in Wangari's backyard failed; almost all the seedlings died. But Wangari was not one to give up, and she showed others how not to give up.

Many of the women could not read or write. They were mothers and farmers, and no one took them seriously.

But they did not need schooling to plant trees. They did not have to wait for the government to help them. They could begin to change their own lives.

All this was heavy work, but the women felt proud. Slowly, all around them, they could begin to see the fruit of the work of their hands. The woods were growing up again. Now when they cut down a tree, they planted two in its place. Their families were healthier, eating from the fruit trees they had planted and from the vegetable plots filled again with the yams, cassava, pigeon peas, and sorghum that grew so well. They had work to do, and the work brought them together as one, like the trees growing together on the newly wooded hills.

The men saw what their wives, mothers, and daughters were doing and admired them and even joined in.

Wangari gave seedlings to the schools and taught the children how to make their own nurseries.

She gave seedlings to inmates of prisons and even to soldiers. "You hold your gun," she told the soldiers, "but what are you protecting? The whole country is disappearing with the wind and water. You should hold the gun in your right hand and a tree seedling in your left. That's when you become a good soldier."

And so in the thirty years since Wangari began her movement, tree by tree, person by person, thirty million trees have been planted in Kenya—and the planting has not stopped.

"When the soil is exposed," Wangari tells us, "it is crying out for help, it is naked and needs to be clothed in its dress. That is the nature of the land. It needs color, it needs its cloth of green."

AUTHOR'S NOTE

In 2004, Wangari Maathai was the first woman from Africa to receive the Nobel Peace Prize. It was awarded to her for the connection she made between the health of her country's natural environment and the well-being of her country's people. In Kenya, where a vast majority of the people depend directly on the land for survival, that connection is glaringly evident.

Wangari Maathai was born in 1940, when Kenya was still a British colony. The daughter of a peasant farmer, she grew up in the Central Highlands, the fertile hill country settled by Europeans after the British built a railroad through the region at the end of the nineteenth century. The foreign settlers took the best lands and established large plantations, using native Kenyans as laborers. Local families farmed the remaining small plots, living off what they grew. This was the Kenya Wangari knew before she left for America to study biology at Mount St. Scholastica College (now called Benedictine College) in Atchison, Kansas.

In 1963, while Wangari was studying in Kansas, Kenya gained its independence from Britain. On her return in 1966, and in the years that followed, Wangari noticed great changes. The population of Kenya was growing rapidly. The land no longer seemed able to feed everyone. Traditional farming methods were often abandoned, small farmers increasingly turned to commercial farming, more and more land was being cleared for crops, and the remaining woods were being cut for household needs. Wangari noticed that there was more poverty than before, more malnutrition, more hunger, and more unemployment.

Kenya's crisis, like that of our planet as a whole, is that of an ever-expanding population dependent on ever-shrinking natural resources. From this realization Wangari Maathai's Green Belt Movement was born.

Founded in 1977, the Green Belt Movement has given many Kenyans purpose and confidence and, through its educational programs, taught them skills and transformed them into active, informed citizens who hold their government accountable for what it does. "I always felt," says Wangari, "that our work was not simply about planting trees. It was about inspiring people to take charge of their environment, the system that governed them, their lives and their future."

There are now nearly one hundred thousand Green Belt Movement members throughout Kenya who, in addition to tending thousands of seedling nurseries, have been inspired to start many local projects. In one village, for example, the Green Belt Movement loans beehives to farmers in exchange for tree planting. When the farmers plant enough trees, they become owners of the hives and can sell their honey for a good price. Female goats are also loaned to farmers. If a goat bears a female kid, and if the farmer gives that kid to another movement member, the farmer becomes the permanent owner of the mother goat, in this way acquiring much-needed livestock. Money never changes hands, and yet, in this simple way, people who are poor can take the first steps toward improving their own lives.

Over the years, Wangari Maathai's work has demanded persistence and courage. In 1989, she angered the government by protesting its plan to build a sixty-two-story building in Uhuru Park in the nation's capital of Nairobi. In retaliation, the government evicted the Green Belt Movement from the headquarters it had occupied for ten years. Wangari's friends were so afraid of what the government might do to her that they moved her from house to house to shelter her. The skyscraper, however, was never built.

In 1999, Wangari and her supporters, armed with seedlings, protested the government's plan to sell off portions of Karura Forest. Security guards awaited the protesters and, in the struggle that followed, Wangari was hurt and hospitalized with head injuries. However, that government scheme, too, was defeated.

Wangari does not think of herself as brave. She simply believes that those who feel strongly about something and understand what needs to be done must act.

Wangari Maathai has been a member of Kenya's Parliament since 2002 and Assistant Minister for Environment in the Ministry of Environment and Natural Resources since 2003. She is the mother of three grown children, Waweru, Wanjira, and Muta.

For Gus, my companion in everything,
for Po and Ney, whom I adore,
and for the three marvelous Sams

Of the many books and other sources I consulted, the following were especially helpful: Wangari Maathai's *The Green Belt Movement: Sharing the Approach and the Experience* (Lantern Books, 2003) and *Unbowed: A Memoir* (Knopf, 2006), and two National Public Radio interviews: "Wangari Maathai" ("The Connection," WBUR Boston, June 21, 2005) and "Wangari Maathai: A Watering Can, Some Seedlings, and the Greening of a Nation" ("Living on Earth," July 1, 2005). I would also like to thank Sister Marie Louise Krenner at Benedictine College, Robin Lubbock at WBUR, and especially Wanjira Mathai and the Green Belt Movement.

Printed in China by South China Printing Co. Ltd.,
Dongguan City, Guangdong Province
Designed by Nancy Goldenberg
First edition, 2008
5   7   9   10   8   6

www.fsgkidsbooks.com

Library of Congress Cataloging-in-Publication Data
Nivola, Claire A.
    Planting the trees of Kenya : the story of Wangari Maathai / Claire A. Nivola.— 1st ed.
        p. cm.
    ISBN 978-0-374-39918-4
    1. Maathai, Wangari—Juvenile literature. 2. Tree planters (Persons)—Kenya—Biography—Juvenile
literature. 3. Green Belt Movement (Society : Kenya)—Juvenile literature. 4. Women conservationists—
Kenya—Biography—Juvenile literature. 5. Women politicians—Kenya—Biography—Juvenile literature.
I. Title.

SB63.M22N58 2008
333.72092—dc22
[B]
                                                                            2006038249

Printed on recycled paper